HUGGY DOLLS 2

Amigurumi Crochet Patterns

SAYJAI THAWORNSUPACHAROEN

From the series : Sayjai's Amigurumi Crochet Patterns, volume 7

K AND J PUBLISHING
16 Whitegate Close, Swavesey, Cambridge CB24 4TT, England

www.facebook.com/kandjdolls.amigurumi.patterns
kandjdolls.blogspot.com

· C O N T E N T S ·

Sayjai Amigurumi

Introduction

Huggy Dolls 2 is a collection of cute, huggable, easy to make dolls. Included are the patterns for small cupcakes, a donut and a baby bottle. The doll patterns are for: a Baby, Clown, Mermaid, Tiger, Lion, Mouse, Lamb, Dog, Long Eared Bunny and 2 Foxes. The crochet stitches used are: single crochet (UK: double crochet), half double crochet (UK: half treble crochet), double crochet (UK: treble crochet) and slip stitch.

In this book the Huggy Dolls are wearing onesies. The pattern for the head shape is identical to the first Huggy Dolls book. If you have the first book, you can make them in onesie style, by using the head pattern from the first book and the body pattern from this book. The doll on the right was made with the head pattern of Huggy Izzy (the first Huggy Dolls book) and the body pattern from this book.

If you also have the first Huggy Dolls books, you can make the dolls from this book with the floppy body from the first book.

Size
● The dolls are 17 to 19.5 inches tall (43 cm to 49.5 cm).

The size of the doll depends on the size of the crochet hook, the thickness of yarn and how you stuff it; a bigger hook and thicker yarn make a bigger doll. A doll stuffed tightly is bigger than a loose stuffed doll.

Abbreviations
This book uses USA crochet terminology.
ch = chain
sc = single crochet
hdc = half double crochet
dc = double crochet
st = stitch
sl = slip
rnd = round
tog = together

Conversion chart for USA/ UK crochet abbreviations:

USA Crochet Abbreviations	UK Crochet Abbreviations
sc = single crochet	dc = double crochet
hdc = half double crochet	htr = half treble crochet
dc = double crochet	tr = treble crochet

How-tos

How to make a magic ring.

Put the yarn end behind the yarn from the ball/ skein to make a loop. Put the hook through the loop and yarn over the hook.

Pull the yarn through the loop.

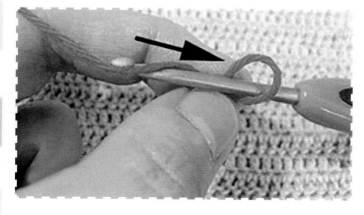

The ring is made.

How to join Yarn.

Join yarn to free loop, ch 1, sc in same st.

How to read pattern.

Rnd 4: (Sc in next 2 sts, 2 sc in next st) around. (24)
Number (24) at the end of round = number of stitches after finished round.

Rnd 5: (Sc in next 3 sts, 2 sc in next st) around. (30)
Repeat (Sc in next 3 sts, 2 sc in next st) until end of round.
=> Rnd 5: (Sc in next 3 sts, 2 sc in next st), (Sc in next 3 sts, 2 sc in next st), (Sc in next 3 sts, 2 sc in next st), (Sc in next 3 sts, 2 sc in next st), (Sc in next 3 sts, 2 sc in next st), (Sc in next 3 sts, 2 sc in next st)
Total stitches of Rnd 5 = 5+5+5+5+5+5 = 30 sts

Rnd 6: Sc in next 2 sts, 2 sc in next st, (sc in next 4 sts, 2 sc in next st) 5 times, sc in next 2 sts. (36)
Repeat (sc in next 4 sts, 2 sc in next st) 5 times.
=> Rnd 6: Sc in next 2 sts, 2 sc in next st, (sc in next 4 sts, 2 sc in next st), (sc in next 4 sts, 2 sc in next st), (sc in next 4 sts, 2 sc in next st), (sc in next 4 sts, 2 sc in next st), (sc in next 4 sts, 2 sc in next st), sc in next 2 sts.
Total stitches of Rnd 6 = 2+2+6+6+6+6+6+2 = 36 sts

How to crochet round 20 of foot.

Round 20 of the foot can be difficult to make. Below is explained in detail how to do round 20 of the foot. You can use this when you make the foot on page 25.

Rnd 20: Working around the edge of foot. Ch 1, sc next 2 sts tog, sc in next st, sc next 2 sts tog; working in ends of rows 14-19, (sc next 2 rows tog) 3 times; working in rnd 13, sc in next st, (sc next 2 sts tog) 2 times, sc in next st; working in ends of rows 15-19, sc in next row, (sc next 2 rows tog) 2 times. (13)

Round 20 is working around the edge of the foot.

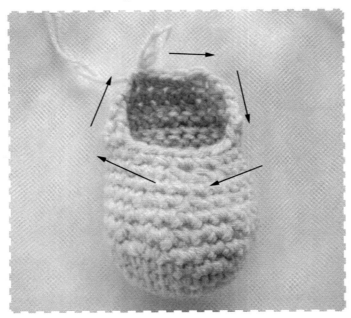

I used **pink yarn** for round 20 so you can see it more clearly. The first 3 sts of rnd 20 is working in row 19: Ch 1, sc next 2 sts tog, sc in next st, sc next 2 sts tog.

The picture below shows the first 3 sts made.

Working in ends of rows 14-19: (sc next 2 rows tog) 3 times. The pictures below show the 4th stitch made.

The pictures below show the 5th stitch made.

The pictures show the 6th stitch made.

Working in round 13: sc in next st, (sc next 2 sts tog) 2 times, sc in next st. The picture shows the 7th stitch made.

This picture shows the 8th stitch made.

The picture below shows 10 stitches made.

10

Working in ends of rows 15-19: sc in next row, (sc next 2 rows tog) 2 times. (Total stitches of round 20 = 13 sts.)
The 2 pictures below show the 11th stitch made:

The pictures below show the 13th stitch made (the last stitch of round 20).

The pictures below & top right show the 12th stitch made.

How to connect legs together.

Rnd 1: Hold 2 legs together, insert the hook through the first leg and pull out the loop from the second leg. Ch 1, sc in same st, sc in next 2 sts. The first 3 sts are working through both legs for joining them together. Do not count these 3 sts. Sc in next 22 sts on **the second leg**, sc in next 22 sts on **the first leg. (44)**

Diagram of how to connect the legs together.

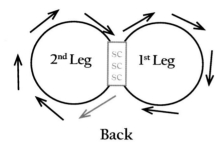

Front

2ⁿᵈ Leg   sc sc sc   1ˢᵗ Leg

Back

The 3 sc stitches are for connecting legs together and go through both legs. The next sc only goes through second leg, then go round.

Step by step:

1) Hold 2 legs together, insert the hook through the first leg and pull out the loop from the second leg.

2) Ch 1, sc in same st, sc in next 2 sts. The first 3 sts are working through both legs for joining them together. Do not count these 3 sts.

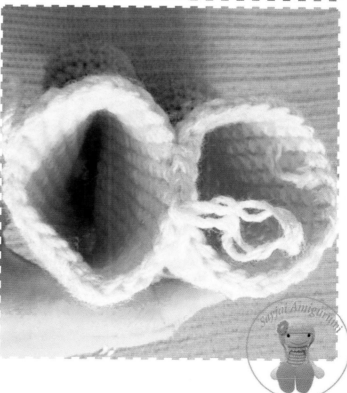

3) Sc in next 22 sts on **the second leg**, sc in next 22 sts on **the first leg**. (44)

The picture below shows the first 3 sts on the second leg. I used red yarn to mark the first st.

The picture below shows the finished round 1 of Huggy Body. I used red yarn to mark the first st.

2nd Leg   1st Leg

Donut

Sew round 1 and round 12 together and stuff polyester fiberfill along while sewing.

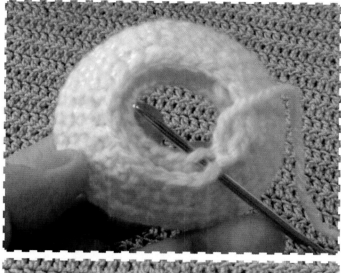

Size

Donut diameter: 2.2 inches or 5.5 cm.

Materials

- DK, Light Worsted
  Sirdar Hayfield Bonus Baby DK color:
  Pastel Pink 866
- 3.00 mm hook
- A little bit of Polyester fiberfill
- Tapestry needle

Donut

Rnd 1: With one strand of **Baby Pink** and 3 mm hook, ch 20, sl st in the first chain to form a ring, ch 1, sc in each ch around. (20)

Rnd 2: (Sc in next 3 sts, 2 sc in next st) around. (25)

Rnd 3: Sc in next 2 sts, 2 sc in next st, (sc in next 4 sts, 2 sc in next st) 4 times, sc in next 2 sts. (30)

Rnd 4: (Sc in next 5 sts, 2 sc in next st) around. (35)

Rnd 5-9: Sc in each st around. (35)

Rnd 10: (Sc next 2 sts tog, sc in next 5 sts) around. (30)

Rnd 11: Sc in next 2 sts, sc next 2 sts tog, (sc in next 4 sts, sc next 2 sts tog) 4 times, sc in next 2 sts. (25)

Rnd 12: (Sc in next 3 sts, sc in next 2 sts tog) around, sl st in first st, leave long end for sewing, fasten off. (20)

Cupcake

Size

The cupcake is 2 inches or 5 cm tall.

Materials

- DK, Light Worsted
  Sirdar Hayfield Bonus Baby DK:
  colors Baby White 856, Baby Mint 853 and
  Pastel Pink 866
  Sirdar Hayfield Bonus DK color Signal Red 977
- 3.00 mm hook
- Polyester fiberfill
- Plastic Pellets
- Tapestry needle

Cup

Rnd 1: With one strand of **Baby Mint** and 3 mm hook,
6 sc in a magic ring. (6)
Rnd 2: 2 sc in each st around. (12)
Rnd 3: (2 sc in next st, sc in next st) around. (18)
Rnd 4: (Sc in next 2 sts, 2 sc in next st) around. (24)
Rnd 5: (2 sc in next st, sc in next 3 sts) around. (30)
Rnd 6: Working in back loops only. Sc in each st around,
changing to **Baby Pink** in last 2 loops of last st. (30)
Rnd 7: Sc in each st around, changing to **Baby Mint** in
last 2 loops of last st.
Rnd 8: Sc in each st around, changing to **Baby Pink** in
last 2 loops of last st. (30)

Rnd 9: Sc in each st around, changing to **Baby Mint** in
last 2 loops of last st. (30)
Rnd 10: Sl st in each st around, leave long end for sewing,
fasten off.

Topping

Row 1: With one strand of **Baby Pink** and 3 mm hook,
ch 10, 2 sc in second ch from hook, sc in next 6 chs,
sc next 2 chs tog, turn. (9)

Rows 2-24 are working in back loops only.

Row 2: Ch 1, sc first 2 sts tog, sc in next 6 sts,
2 sc in next st, changing to **White** in last 2 loops of last
st, turn. (9)
Row 3: Ch 1, 2 sc in first st, sc in next 6 sts, sc next 2 sts
tog, turn. (9)
Row 4: Ch 1, sc first 2 sts tog, sc in next 6 sts, 2 sc in
next st, changing to **Baby Pink** in last 2 loops of last st,
turn. (9)

Repeat rows 3-4 and change color every 2 rows, fasten off
after finished row 24.

Sew the first row and the last row together.

Sew the topping to the cup.

Stuff the cup with plastic pellets and put polyester fiberfill on top, sew the opening close.

Cherry

Rnd 1: With 1 strand of **Red** and 3 mm hook, 6 sc in a magic ring. (6)
Rnd 2: 2 sc in each st around. (12)
Rnd 3: Sc in each st around. (12)
Rnd 4: Sc next 2 sts tog around, sl st in first st, leave long end for sewing, fasten off. Stuff the cherry.

Sew the opening close then sew the cherry on top.

Baby Bottle

Size

The Baby Bottle is 3.6 inches or 9 cm tall.

Materials

- DK, Light Worsted [3 Light]
  Sirdar Hayfield Bonus Baby DK: a little bit of color Baby White 856 and Baby Blue 854
- 5.00 mm hook
- Polyester fiberfill
- Tapestry needle

Bottle

Rnd 1: With 2 strands of **Baby White** and 5 mm hook, 6 sc in a magic ring. (6)
Rnd 2-3: Sc in each st around. (6)
Rnd 4: 2 sc in each st around. (12)
Rnd 5: (Sc in next st, 2 sc in next st) around. (18)
Rnd 6: Sc in each st around, changing to **Baby Blue** in last 2 loops of last st. (18)
Rnd 7: Sc in each st around. (18)
Rnd 8: Working in back loops only. Sc in each st around.
Rnd 9-16: Sc in each st around. Stuff.
Rnd 17: Working in back loops only. (Sc next 2 sts tog, sc in next st) around. (12)
Rnd 18: Sc next 2 sts tog around, sl st in first st, leave long end for sewing, fasten off. (6)
Sew the opening close.

Mr & Mrs Fox

Size

Mr and Mrs Fox are 17 inches (43 cm) tall, excluding ears.

Materials

- DK, Light Worsted
  Sirdar Hayfield Bonus DK: Chocolate 947 = 35 g,
  Black 965 = 25 g, Iced Pink 958 (Light Pink) = 50 g,
  Fox 779 = 140 g, White 961 = 10 g and
  Fluoro 737 (Dark Pink) = 45 g
- 5.00 mm hook (US: H/8, UK: 6)
- Tapestry needle
- Pins
- 2 pair of 12mm safety eyes
- Polyester fibrefill = 290 g for 2 dolls

Remarks

- This project is working in continuous rounds, do not join or turn unless otherwise stated. Mark first stitch of each round.
- Crochet using 2 strands of yarn.
- The Foxes have the same basic patterns: Head, Ears, Arms, Tail, Snout, Collar and Cuff.

Basic Patterns

Head

Rnd 1: With 2 strands of **Fox 779** (skin color) and 5 mm hook, 6 sc in a magic ring. (6)
Rnd 2: 2 sc in each st around. (12)
Rnd 3: (2 sc in next st, sc in next st) around. (18)
Rnd 4: (Sc in next 2 sts, 2 sc in next st) around. (24)
Rnd 5: (Sc in next 3 sts, 2 sc in next st) around. (30)
Rnd 6: Sc in next 2 sts, 2 sc in next st, (sc in next 4 sts, 2 sc in next st) 5 times, sc in next 2 sts. (36)
Rnd 7: (Sc in next 5 sts, 2 sc in next st) around. (42)
Rnd 8: Sc in next 3 sts, 2 sc in next st, (sc in next 6 sts, 2 sc in next st) 5 times, sc in next 3 sts. (48)
Rnd 9-14: Sc in each st around. (48)
Rnd 15: Sc in next 3 sts, sc next 2 sts tog, (sc in next 6 sts, sc next 2 sts tog) 5 times, sc in next 3 sts. (42)
Rnd 16: Sc in each st around.
Rnd 17: (Sc next 2 sts tog, sc in next 5 sts) around. (36)
Rnd 18: Sc in each st around. (36)

Rnd 19: Sc in next 2 sts, sc next 2 sts tog, (sc in next 4 sts, sc next 2 sts tog) 5 times, sc in next 2 sts. (30)
Rnd 20: Sc in each st around. (30)
Rnd 21: (Sc in next 3 sts, sc next 2 sts tog) around. (24)
Rnd 22: Sc in each st around. (24)
Rnd 23: (Sc in next 2 sts, sc next 2 sts tog) around. (18)
Rnd 24: Sc in each st around, join with sl st in first st, fasten off. (18)

Stuff head a little bit, insert safety eyes 4-5 sts apart between rnds 16-17 of head then stuff head more tightly.

Arm

Make 2.
Rnd 1: With 2 strands of **Fox 779** (skin color) and 5 mm hook, 6 sc in a magic ring. (6)
Rnd 2: 2 sc in each st around. (12)
Rnd 3: (Sc in next st, 2 sc in next st) around. (18)
Rnd 4-6: Sc in each st around.
Rnd 7: (Sc next 2 sts tog, sc in next 4 sts) around. (15)
Rnd 8: (Sc in next 3 sts, sc next 2 sts tog) around. (12)
Rnd 9: (Sc in next 2 sts, sc next 2 sts tog) around, changing to **Iced Pink 958** in last two loops of last st, stuff hand. (9)
Rnd 10-26: Sc in each st around.
Rnd 27: Sc in each st around, join with sl st in first st. Leave long end for sewing, fasten off. Stuff arm but not to tight, so the arm can be flexible. Sew the opening of arm close flat.

Tail

Rnd 1: With 2 strands of **White 961** and 5 mm hook, 6 sc in a magic ring. (6)
Rnd 2: (Sc in next st, 2 sc in next st) around. (9)
Rnd 3: (2 sc in next st, sc in next 2 sts) around. (12)
Rnd 4: (Sc in next 3 sts, 2 sc in next st) around. (15)
Rnd 5: Sc in next 2 sts, 2 sc in next st, (sc in next 4 sts, 2 sc in next st) 2 times, sc in next 2 sts. (18)
Rnd 6: Sc in each st around.
Rnd 7: Sc in each st around, changing to **Fox 779** in last two loops of last st.
Rnd 8-11: Sc in each st around.
Rnd 12: Sc in next 2 sts, sc next 2 sts tog, (sc in next 4 sts, sc next 2 sts tog) 2 times, sc in next 2 sts. (15)
Rnd 13-14: Sc in each st around.
Rnd 15: (Sc in next 3 sts, sc next 2 sts tog) around. (12)
Rnd 16-17: Sc in each st around. Stuff tail.
Rnd 18: (Sc in next 2 sts, sc next 2 sts tog) around. (9)
Rnd 19-20: Sc in each st around.
Rnd 21: (Sc in next st, sc next 2 sts tog) around. (6)
Rnd 22: Sc in each st around.
Rnd 23: Sc in each st around, join with sl st in first st. Leave long end for sewing, fasten off. Stuff tail and sew the opening close flat.

Snout

Rnd 1: With 2 strands of **Black 965** and 5 mm hook, 4 sc in a magic ring, changing to **White 961** in last two loops of last st. (4)
Rnd 2: 2 sc in next 2 sts, sc in next 2 sts. (6)
Rnd 3: Sc in next st, 2 sc in next 2 sts, sc in next st, sc next 2 sts tog. (7)
Rnd 4: Sc next 2 sts tog, 2 sc in next 2 sts, sc next 2 sts tog, sc in next st, join with sl st in first st, leave long end for sewing, fasten off. (7)

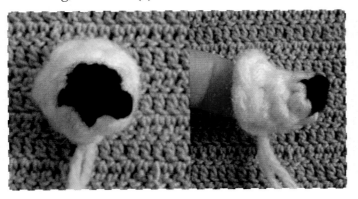

Ear

Make 2.
Rnd 1: With 2 strands of **Black 965** and 5 mm hook, 4 sc in a magic ring. (4)
Rnd 2: (Sc in next st, 2 sc in next st) 2 times, changing to **Fox 779** in last two loops of last st. (6)
Rnd 3: Sc in each st around. (6)
Rnd 4: (Sc in next st, 2 sc in next st) around. (9)
Rnd 5: (2 sc in next st, sc in next 2 sts) around. (12)
Rnd 6: (Sc in next 3 sts, 2 sc in next st) around. (15)
Rnd 7: Sc in each st around. (15)
Rnd 8: (Sc next 2 sts tog, sc in next 3 sts), join with sl st in first st, fasten off. (12)
Sew the opening of the ear close flat.

Collar

With 2 strands of **Iced Pink 958** and 5 mm hook, ch 22, sc in second chain from hook, sc in next 20 chs, leave long end for sewing, fasten off. (21)

Cuff

With 2 strands of **Iced Pink 958** and 5 mm hook, ch 14, sc in second chain from hook, sc in next 12 chs, leave long end for sewing, fasten off. (13)

Mrs Fox

Head

Make one same as basic head pattern on page 17.

Body

Rnd 1: With 2 strands of **Fluoro 737** (pants color) and 5 mm hook, 6 sc in a magic ring. (6)
Rnd 2: 2 sc in each st around. (12)
Rnd 3: (2 sc in next st, sc in next st) around. (18)
Rnd 4: (Sc in next 2 sts, 2 sc in next st) around. (24)
Rnd 5: (Sc in next 3 sts, 2 sc in next st) around. (30)
Rnd 6: Sc in next 2 sts, 2 sc in next st, (sc in next 4 sts, 2 sc in next st) 5 times, sc in next 2 sts. (36)
Rnd 7-8: Sc in each st around.
Rnd 9: Sc in each st around, changing to **Iced Pink 958** in last two loops of last st.
Rnd 10: <u>Working in back loops only.</u> Sc in each st around, changing to **Fluoro** in last two loops of last st.
Rnd 11: Sc in next 5 sts, sc next 2 sts tog, (sc in next 10 sts, sc next 2 sts tog) 2 times, sc in next 5 sts, changing to **Iced Pink** in last two loops of last st. (33)
Rnd 12: Sc in each st around, changing to **Fluoro** in last two loops of last st.
Rnd 13: Sc in each st around, changing to **Iced Pink** in last two loops of last st.
Rnd 14: (Sc next 2 sts tog, sc in next 9 sts) around, changing to **Fluoro** in last two loops of last st.(30)
Rnd 15: Sc in each st around, changing to **Iced Pink** in last two loops of last st. (30)
Rnd 16: Sc in each st around, changing to **Fluoro** in last two loops of last st. (30)
Rnd 17: Sc in next 4 sts, sc next 2 sts tog, (sc in next 8 sts, sc next 2 sts tog) 2 times, sc in next 4 sts, changing to **Iced Pink** in last two loops of last st. (27)
Rnd 18: Sc in each st around, changing to **Fluoro** in last two loops of last st.
Rnd 19: Sc in each st around, changing to **Iced Pink** in last two loops of last st.
Rnd 20: (Sc next 2 sts tog, sc in next 7 sts) around, changing to **Fluoro** in last two loops of last st. (24)
Rnd 21: Sc in each st around, changing to **Iced Pink** in last two loops of last st.
Rnd 22: Sc in next 3 sts, sc next 2 sts tog, (sc in next 6 sts, sc next 2 sts tog) 2 times, sc in next 3 sts. (21)
Rnd 23: Sc in each st around.
Rnd 24: (Sc next 2 sts tog, sc in next 5 sts) around. (18)
Rnd 25-26: Sc in each st around.
Rnd 27: Sc in each st around, join with sl st in first st, leave long end for sewing, fasten off.

Skirt

Rnd 1: With 2 strands of **Fluoro**, join yarn to free loop of rnd 9, ch 1, sc in same st, sc in each st around, changing to **Iced Pink** in last two loops of last st. (36)

Rnd 2: (Sc in next 11 sts, 2 sc in next st) around, changing to **Fluoro** in last two loops of last st. (39)
Rnd 3: Sc in each st around, changing to **Iced Pink** in last two loops of last st.
Rnd 4: Sc in each st around, changing to **Fluoro** in last two loops of last st.
Rnd 5: Sc in next 6 sts, 2 sc in next st, (sc in next 12 sts, 2 sc in next st) 2 times, sc in next 6 sts, changing to **Iced Pink** in last two loops of last st. (42)
Rnd 6: Sc in each st around, changing to **Fluoro** in last two loops of last st.
Rnd 7: Sc in each st around, changing to **Iced Pink** in last two loops of last st.
Rnd 8: (Sc in next 13 sts, 2 sc in next st) around, changing to **Fluoro** in last two loops of last st. (45)
Rnd 9: Sc in each st around, join with sl st in first st, leave long end for sewing, fasten off.

Stuff the body and sew to head.

Foot and Leg

Make 2.
Rnd 1: With 2 strands of **Fluoro 737** (shoe color) and 5 mm hook, 6 sc in a magic ring. (6)
Rnd 2: 2 sc in each st around. (12)
Rnd 3: (Sc in next st, 2 sc in next st) around. (18)
Rnd 4: (2 sc in next st, sc in next 2 sts) around. (24)
Rnd 5: Sc in each st around. (24)
Rnd 6: (Sc in next 7 sts, 2 sc in next st) around. (27)
Rnd 7: Sc in next 4 sts, 2 sc in next st, (sc in next 8 sts, 2 sc in next st) 2 times, sc in next 4 sts. (30)
Rnd 8: Sc in next 17 sts, sc next 2 sts tog, (sc in next 2 sts, sc next 2 sts tog) 2 times, sc in next 3 sts. (27)
Rnd 9: Sc in each st around. (27)
Rnd 10: Sc in next 16 sts, sc next 2 sts tog, (sc in next st, sc next 2 sts tog) 2 times, sc in next 3 sts. (24)
Rnd 11: Sc in each st around. (24)
Rnd 12: Sc in next 15 sts, (sc next 2 sts tog) 3 times, sc in next 3 sts. (21)
Rnd 13: Sc in each st around. (21)

Rows 14-19: Working in rows.
Row 14: Sc in next 15 sts, turn. (15)
Row 15: Ch 1, sc first 2 sts tog, sc in next 11 sts, sc next 2 sts tog, turn. (13)
Row 16: Ch 1, sc first 2 sts tog, sc in next 9 sts, sc next 2 sts tog, turn. (11)
Row 17: Ch 1, sc first 2 sts tog, sc in next 7 sts, sc next 2 sts tog, turn. (9)
Row 18: Ch 1, sc first 2 sts tog, sc in next 5 sts, sc next 2 sts tog, turn. (7)
Row 19: Ch 1, sc first 2 sts tog, sc in next 3 sts, sc next 2 sts tog, turn. (5)

Rounds 20-40 are working in rounds.
Rnd 20: Working around the edge of foot.
Ch 1, sc next 2 sts tog, sc in next st, sc next 2 sts tog; working in ends of rows 14-19, (sc next 2 rows tog) 3 times; working in rnd 13, sc in next st, (sc next 2 sts tog) 2 times, sc in next st; working in ends of rows 15-19, sc in next row, (sc next 2 rows tog) 2 times, changing to **Fox 779** (skin color) in last three loops of last st. (13)
See how to crochet round 20 on page 8.

Rnd 21: Sc in next st, sc in next 2 sts tog, sc in next 3 sts, (sc next 2 sts tog) 2 times, sc in next 3 sts. Stuff. (10)
Rnd 22-39: Sc in each st around.
Rnd 40: Sc in each st around, sl st in first st, leave long end for sewing, fasten off. Stuff legs a little bit and not too tight. Sew the opening close flat.

Sew legs to body on rnds 1-4.

Make a Tail, a Snout, 2 Arms, 2 Ears, a Collar and 2 cuffs, see patterns on page 17-18.

Finishing

Sew arms on rnd 24 of the body.

Sew collar around the neck and cuffs around the wrists.

Pin snout between eyes on rnds 17-19 and sew.

Pin ears on rnds 4-9 of head and sew.

Sew tail on rnd 10 of the body.

Mr Fox

Head
Make one the same as the basic head pattern on page 17.

Body
Rnd 1: With 2 strands of **Chocolate 947** (pants color) and 5 mm hook, 6 sc in a magic ring. (6)
Rnd 2: 2 sc in each st around. (12)
Rnd 3: (2 sc in next st, sc in next st) around. (18)
Rnd 4: (Sc in next 2 sts, 2 sc in next st) around. (24)
Rnd 5: (Sc in next 3 sts, 2 sc in next st) around. (30)
Rnd 6: Sc in next 2 sts, 2 sc in next st, (sc in next 4 sts, 2 sc in next st) 5 times, sc in next 2 sts. (36)
Rnd 7-8: Sc in each st around.
Rnd 9: Sc in each st around, changing to **Iced Pink 958** in last two loops of last st.
Rnd 10: Sc in each st around.
Rnd 11: (Sc next 2 sts tog, sc in next 10 sts) around. (33)
Rnd 12-13: Sc in each st around.
Rnd 14: (Sc next 2 sts tog, sc in next 9 sts) around. (30)
Rnd 15-16: Sc in each st around.
Rnd 17: Sc in next 4 sts, sc next 2 sts tog, (sc in next 8 sts, sc next 2 sts tog) 2 times, sc in next 4 sts. (27)
Rnd 18-19: Sc in each st around.
Rnd 20: (Sc next 2 sts tog, sc in next 7 sts) around. (24)
Rnd 21: Sc in each st around.
Rnd 22: Sc in next 3 sts, sc next 2 sts tog, (sc in next 6 sts, sc next 2 sts tog) 2 times, sc in next 3 sts. (21)
Rnd 23: Sc in each st around.
Rnd 24: (Sc next 2 sts tog, sc in next 5 sts) around. (18)
Rnd 25-26: Sc in each st around.
Rnd 27: Sc in each st around, leave long end for sewing, fasten off.
Stuff the body and sew to head.

Foot and Leg
Make 2.
Rnd 1: With 2 strands of **Black 965** (shoe color) and 5 mm hook, 6 sc in a magic ring. (6)
Rnd 2: 2 sc in each st around. (12)
Rnd 3: (Sc in next st, 2 sc in next st) around. (18)
Rnd 4: (2 sc in next st, sc in next 2 sts) around. (24)
Rnd 5: Sc in each st around. (24)
Rnd 6: (Sc in next 7 sts, 2 sc in next st) around. (27)
Rnd 7: Sc in next 4 sts, 2 sc in next st, (sc in next 8 sts, 2 sc in next st) 2 times, sc in next 4 sts. (30)
Rnd 8: Sc in next 17 sts, sc next 2 sts tog, (sc in next 2 sts, sc next 2 sts tog) 2 times, sc in next 3 sts. (27)
Rnd 9: Sc in each st around. (27)
Rnd 10: Sc in next 16 sts, sc next 2 sts tog, (sc in next st, sc next 2 sts tog) 2 times, sc in next 3 sts. (24)
Rnd 11: Sc in each st around. (24)
Rnd 12: Sc in next 15 sts, (sc next 2 sts tog) 3 times, sc in next 3 sts. (21)
Rnd 13: Sc in each st around. (21)

Rows 14-19: Working in Rows.
Row 14: Sc in next 15 sts, turn. (15)
Row 15: Ch 1, sc first 2 sts tog, sc in next 11 sts, sc next 2 sts tog, turn. (13)
Row 16: Ch 1, sc first 2 sts tog, sc in next 9 sts, sc next 2 sts tog, turn. (11)
Row 17: Ch 1, sc first 2 sts tog, sc in next 7 sts, sc next 2 sts tog, turn. (9)
Row 18: Ch 1, sc first 2 sts tog, sc in next 5 sts, sc next 2 sts tog, turn. (7)
Row 19: Ch 1, sc first 2 sts tog, sc in next 3 sts, sc next 2 sts tog, turn. (5)

Rounds 20-40 are working in rounds.
Rnd 20: Working around the edge of foot.
Ch 1, sc next 2 sts tog, sc in next st, sc next 2 sts tog; working in ends of rows 14-19, (sc next 2 rows tog) 3 times; working in rnd 13, sc in next st, (sc next 2 sts tog) 2 times, sc in next st; working in ends of rows 15-19, sc in next row, (sc next 2 rows tog) 2 times, changing to **Chocolate 947** (pants color) in last three loops of last st. (13) See how to crochet round 20 on page 8.
Rnd 21-39: Sc in each st around. (13)

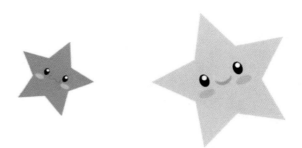

Rnd 40: Sc in each st around, sl st in first st, leave long end for sewing, fasten off.

Stuff legs a little bit, not too tight. Sew the opening close flat. Sew legs to body on rnds 1-5.

Belt

With 2 strands of **Chocolate 947** and 5 mm hook, ch 40, sc in second chain from hook, sc in next 38 chs, leave long end for sewing, fasten off. (39)

Make a Tail, a Snout, 2 Arms, 2 Ears, a Collar and 2 Cuffs, see patterns on page 17-18.

Finishing

Sew arms on rnd 24 of the body.
Sew collar around the neck and cuffs around the wrists.
Pin snout between eyes on rnds 17-19 and sew.
Pin ears on rnds 4-9 of head and sew.
Sew tail on rnd 8 of the body.
Sew belt around the body on rnds 9-10, embroider a buckle with one strand of **Fox 779**.

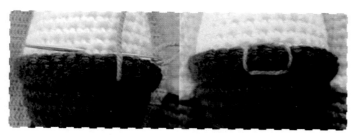

Huggy Dolls

Basic Patterns

Huggy Head

Rnd 1: With 2 strands of **Cream** and 5 mm hook,
6 sc in a magic ring. (6)
Rnd 2: 2 sc in each st around. (12)
Rnd 3: (2 sc in next st, sc in next st) around. (18)
Rnd 4: (Sc in next 2 sts, 2 sc in next st) around. (24)
Rnd 5: (Sc in next 3 sts, 2 sc in next st) around. (30)
Rnd 6: Sc in next 2 sts, 2 sc in next st, (sc in next 4 sts,
2 sc in next st) 5 times, sc in next 2 sts. (36)
Rnd 7: (Sc in next 5 sts, 2 sc in next st) around. (42)
Rnd 8: Sc in next 3 sts, 2 sc in next st, (sc in next 6 sts,
2 sc in next st) 5 times, sc in next 3 sts. (48)
Rnd 9: (Sc in next 7 sts, 2 sc in next st) around. (54)
Rnd 10: Sc in next 4 sts, 2 sc in next st, (sc in next 8 sts,
2 sc in next st) 5 times, sc in next 4 sts. (60)
Rnd 11-16: Sc in each st around.
Rnd 17: (Sc next 2 sts tog, sc in next 8 sts) around. (54)
Rnd 18: (Sc in next 7 sts, sc next 2 sts tog) around. (48)
Rnd 19: Sc in next 3 sts, sc next 2 sts tog, (sc in next 6
sts, sc next 2 sts tog) 5 times, sc in next 3 sts. (42)
Rnd 20: (Sc in next 5 sts, sc next 2 sts tog) around. (36)
Rnd 21: Sc in next 2 sts, sc next 2 sts tog, (sc in next 4
sts, sc next 2 sts tog) 5 times, sc in next 2 sts. (30)
Rnd 22: (Sc in next 3 sts, sc next 2 sts tog) around. (24)
Rnd 23: (Sc in next 2 sts, sc next 2 sts tog) around,
join with sl st in first st, fasten off. (18)
Stuff head a little bit, insert safety eyes 10 sts apart
between rnds 13-14 of head then stuff head more tightly.

Huggy Foot and Leg

Make 2.
Rnd 1: With 2 strands of **Bluebell 969** (foot color) and
5 mm hook, 6 sc in a magic ring. (6)
Rnd 2: 2 sc in each st around. (12)
Rnd 3: (Sc in next st, 2 sc in next st) around. (18)
Rnd 4: (2 sc in next st, sc in next 2 sts) around. (24)
Rnd 5: Sc in each st around. (24)
Rnd 6: (Sc in next 7 sts, 2 sc in next st) around. (27)
Rnd 7: Sc in next 4 sts, 2 sc in next st, (sc in next 8 sts,
2 sc in next st) 2 times, sc in next 4 sts. (30)
Rnd 8: Sc in next 17 sts, sc next 2 sts tog, (sc in next 2
sts, sc next 2 sts tog) 2 times, sc in next 3 sts. (27)
Rnd 9: Sc in each st around. (27)
Rnd 10: Sc in next 16 sts, sc next 2 sts tog, (sc in next st,
sc next 2 sts tog) 2 times, sc in next 3 sts. (24)
Rnd 11: Sc in each st around. (24)
Rnd 12: Sc in next 15 sts, (sc next 2 sts tog) 3 times,
sc in next 3 sts. (21)
Rnd 13: Sc in each st around. (21)

Rows 14-19 are working in rows.
Row 14: Sc in next 15 sts, turn. (15)
Row 15: Ch 1, sc first 2 sts tog, sc in next 11 sts,
sc next 2 sts tog, turn. (13)
Row 16: Ch 1, sc first 2 sts tog, sc in next 9 sts,
sc next 2 sts tog, turn. (11)
Row 17: Ch 1, sc first 2 sts tog, sc in next 7 sts,
sc next 2 sts tog, turn. (9)
Row 18: Ch 1, sc first 2 sts tog, sc in next 5 sts,
sc next 2 sts tog, turn. (7)
Row 19: Ch 1, sc first 2 sts tog, sc in next 3 sts,
sc next 2 sts tog, turn. (5)

Rounds 20-40 are working in rounds.

Rnd 20: Working around the edge of foot. Ch 1, sc next 2 sts tog, sc in next st, sc next 2 sts tog; working in ends of rows 14-19, (sc next 2 rows tog) 3 times; working in rnd 13, sc in next st, (sc next 2 sts tog) 2 times, sc in next st; working in ends of rows 15-19, sc in next row, (sc next 2 rows tog) 2 times. (13)
See how to crochet round 20 on page 8.

Rnd 21: Sc in next st, sc in next 2 sts tog, sc in next 3 sts, (sc next 2 sts tog) 2 times, sc in next 3 sts, changing to **Baby Blue 854** (pants color) in last 2 loops of last st. Stuff foot. (10)
Rnd 22: 2 sc in each st around. (20)
Rnd 23: (Sc in next 3 sts, 2 sc in next st) around. (25)
Rnd 24-40: Sc in each st around.
Rnd 41: Sc in each st around.

The first leg: join with sl st in first st, fasten off.
The second leg: do not sl st in first st, do not fasten off.

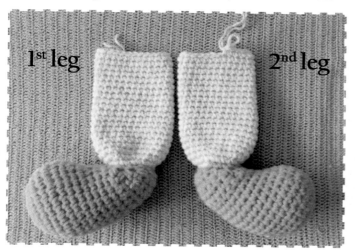

1st leg   2nd leg

Huggy Body

Rnd 1: Hold 2 legs together, insert the hook through the first leg and pull out the loop from the second leg. Ch 1, sc in same st, sc in next 2 sts. The first 3 sts are working through both legs for joining them together. Do not count these 3 sts. Sc in next 22 sts on **the second leg**, sc in next 22 sts on **the first leg**. (44)
See how to crochet round 1 of the body on page 11.
Rnd 2-13: Sc in each st around. Stuff legs.
Rnd 14: (Sc in next 9 sts, sc next 2 sts tog) around. (40)
Rnd 15-16: Sc in each st around.
Rnd 17: Sc in next 4 sts, sc next 2 sts tog, (sc in next 8 sts, sc next 2 sts tog) 3 times, sc in next 4 sts. (36)
Rnd 18-19: Sc in each st around.
Rnd 20: (Sc in next 7 sts, sc next 2 sts tog) around. (32)
Rnd 21: Sc in each st around.
Rnd 22: Sc in next 3 sts, sc next 2 sts tog, (sc in next 6 sts, sc next 2 sts tog) 3 times, sc in next 3 sts. (28)
Rnd 23: Sc in each st around.

Rnd 24: (Sc in next 5 sts, sc next 2 sts tog) around. (24)
Rnd 25: Sc in each st around.
Rnd 26: (Sc in next 2 sts, sc next 2 sts tog) around, join with sl st in first st, leave long end for sewing, fasten off. (18) Stuff body.

Tip for stuffing basic Huggy Dolls

Head : 100 g of polyester filling, stuff head tightly.
Foot : 15 g of polyester filling for one foot.
Leg : 20 g of polyester filling for one leg.
Body : 60 g of polyester filling.
Hand & Arm : 10 g of polyester filling for one hand & arm.

26

Sew body to the head.

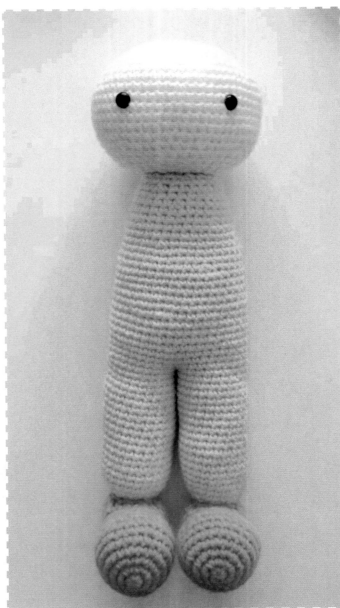

Arm
Make 2.

Rnd 1: With 2 strands of **Cream** (hand color) and 5 mm hook, 6 sc in a magic ring. (6)
Rnd 2: 2 sc in each st around. (12)
Rnd 3: (Sc in next st, 2 sc in next st) around. (18)
Rnd 4-6: Sc in each st around.
Rnd 7: (Sc next 2 sts tog, sc in next 4 sts) around. (15)
Rnd 8: (Sc in next 3 sts, sc next 2 sts tog) around. (12)
Rnd 9: (Sc next 2 sts tog, sc in next 2 sts) around, changing to **Baby Blue 854** (sleeves color) in last 2 loops of last st. Stuff hand. (9)
Rnd 10: 2 sc in each st around. (18)
Rnd 11-16: Sc in each st around.
Rnd 17: Sc next 2 sts tog, sc in next 16 sts. Stuff. (17)
Rnd 18: Sc in next 8 sts, sc next 2 sts tog, sc in next 7 sts. (16)
Rnd 19: Sc in next 3 sts, sc next 2 sts tog, sc in next 11 sts. (15)
Rnd 20: Sc in next 11 sts, sc next 2 sts tog, sc in next 2 sts. (14)
Rnd 21: Sc next 2 sts tog, sc in next 12 sts. (13)
Rnd 22: Sc in next 3 sts, sc next 2 sts tog, sc in next 8 sts. (12)
Rnd 23: Sc in next 6 sts, sc next 2 sts tog, sc in next 4 sts. (11)
Rnd 24: Sc in next 2 sts, sc next 2 sts tog, sc in next 7 sts. (10)
Rnd 25: Sc in next 4 sts, sc next 2 sts tog, sc in next 4 sts. (9)
Rnd 26: Sc in each st around. (9)
Rnd 27: Sc in each st around, join with sl st in first st. Leave long end for sewing, fasten off. Stuff.
Sew arms to body on rnd 25.

Collar

Rows 2-48 are working in back loops only.

Row 1: With 2 strands of **Baby Blue 854** and 5 mm hook. Ch 5, sc in second ch from hook, sc in each st across, turn. (4)

Row 2-47: Ch 1, sc in each st across, turn.

Row 48: Ch 1, sc in each st across, leave long end for sewing, fasten off.

Sew running stitches along the edge to be gathered. Pull gently to slide the collar in small folds to fit the neck. Then sew it around the neck.

Animal Nose

Rnd 1: With DMC Pearl Cotton Thread Size 3 and 3 mm hook, ch 3, sc in second chain from hook, 3 sc in next ch; working in remaining loops on opposite side of chain, 2 sc in next ch. (6)

```
        X    X    O
     X    O    O    X
        X    X
   o = chain       x = sc
```

Rnd 2: Sl st in each st around, leave long end for sewing, fasten off. (6)

Sew nose on rnd 14 between eyes.

Huggy Baby

Size
The Huggy Babies are 17.7 inches (45 cm) tall.

Materials
For making the Blue Huggy Baby:

- DK, Light Worsted
  Sirdar Hayfield Bonus Baby DK, colors
  Baby Cream 855 = 50 g and Baby Blue 854 = 160 g.
  Sirdar Hayfield Bonus DK, color Bluebell 969 = 30 g.
- 5.00 mm hook (US: H/8, UK: 6)
- Tapestry needle
- Polyester fibrefill = 250 g
- One pair of 12mm safety eyes
- 5.5 cm Knitpro Pom Pom maker

Head
With **Baby Cream 855**, make one head the same as the basic Huggy Head pattern on page 24.

Foot and Leg
Make 2 the same as the basic Huggy Foot and Leg pattern on pages 24-25.
Rnds 1-21: color **Bluebell 969**
Rnds 22-41: color **Baby Blue 854**

Body
With **Baby Blue 854**, same as the basic Huggy Body pattern on page 25.

Arm
Make 2 same as basic Huggy Arm pattern on page 26.
Rnds 1-9: color **Baby Cream 855**
Rnds 10-27: color **Baby Blue 854**

Collar
With **Baby Blue 854**, same as Collar pattern on page 27.

Hat
Rows 2-44 are working in back loops only.
Row 1: With 2 strands of **Baby Blue 854** and 5 mm hook, ch 30, 2 sc in second ch from hook, sc in next 26 chs, sc next 2 chs tog, turn. (29)
Row 2: Ch 1, sc first 2 sts tog, sc in next 26 sts, 2 sc in next st, turn. (29)
Row 3: Ch 1, 2 sc in first st, sc in next 26 sts, sc next 2 sts tog, turn. (29)

Repeat rows 2-3 until finished row 44, leave long end for sewing, fasten off.

Fold the hat, sew row 1 and row 44 together then sew the top of hat together flat.

Use Pom Pom maker to make 2 Pom Poms in **Baby Blue** color and attach them to the top of hat.

Put the hat on head and sew to head.

Pink Huggy Baby

Yarn
- Sirdar Hayfield Bonus Baby DK color Pastel Pink 866
- Sirdar Hayfield Bonus DK color Cupid 944, Pink 992 and Cream 812

Head
With **Cream 812** color, make one same as basic Huggy Head pattern on page 24.

Foot and Leg
Make 2 same as basic Huggy Foot and Leg pattern on pages 24-25.
Rnds 1-21: Color **Cupid 944** for the foot.
Rnds 22-41: The main color is **Pastel Pink 866** and has darker pink stripes (color **Pink 992**) on rnds 24, 27, 30, 33, 36 and 39.

Body
Same as basic Huggy Body pattern on page 25.
The main color is **Pastel Pink 866** and has darker pink stripes (color **Pink 992**) on rnds 1, 4, 7, 10, 13, 16, 19, 22 and 25.

Arm
Make 2 same as basic Huggy Arm pattern on page 26.
Rnds 1-9: color **Cream 812**.
Rnds 10-27: The main color is **Pastel Pink 866** color and has darker pink stripes (color **Pink 992**) on rnds 12, 15, 18, 21, 24 and 27.

Collar
With **Pink 992** color, same as Collar pattern on page 27.

Hat
Same as the Hat pattern for the Blue Baby on page 29.
With colors **Pastel Pink 866** and **Pink 992**, changing color in every 2 rows.

Huggy Clown

Size

The Huggy Clown is 19 inches (48 cm) tall.
This includes the hat.

Materials

- DK, Light Worsted
  Sirdar Hayfield Bonus Baby DK color:
  Baby Blue 854 = 20 g, Baby Mint 853 = 40 g,
  Baby Lemon 852 = 85 g, Baby White 856 = 50 g and
  a little bit of Pastel Pink 866
  Sirdar Hayfield Bonus DK color Signal Red 977 = 10 g
- Super Bulky or Super Chunky for the hair,
  brand: Ice yarn Long Eyelash,
  color: Turquoise = 50 g
- 5.00 mm hook (US: H/8, UK: 6)
- Tapestry needle
- Needle and thread for sewing the hair to head
- Polyester fibrefill = 280 g
- One pair of 12mm safety eyes

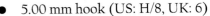

Head

With **Baby White 856**, make one the same as the basic
Huggy Head pattern on page 24.

Hair

Row 1: With Long Eyelash color **Turquoise** (hair color)
and 5 mm hook, ch 35, sc in second chain from hook,
sc in next 33 chs across, turn. (34 sc made)
Row 2-5: Ch 1, sc in each st across, turn. (34)
Row 6: Ch 1, sc in each st across, ch 100, fasten off.
(34 sts, 100 chs)

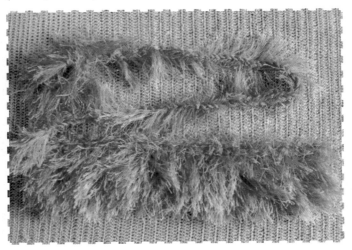

Pin last row of hair on rnd 9 of head and sew.

Pin the rest of chain on rnd 8 – 7 of head and sew. It is
easier to do it one round at a time.

Front

Back

Side

Sayjai Amigurumi

Hat

Rnd 1: With **Baby Mint 853**, 6 sc in a magic ring. (6)
Rnd 2: 2 sc in each st around. (12)
Rnd 3: (Sc in next st, 2 sc in next st) around. (18)
Rnd 4: (2 sc in next st, sc in next 2 sts) around. (24)
Rnd 5: (Sc in next 3 sts, 2 sc in next st) around. (30)
Rnd 6: Sc in next 2 sts, 2 sc in next st, (sc in next 4 sts, 2 sc in next st) 5 times, sc in next 2 sts. (36)
Rnd 7: (Sc in next 5 sts, 2 sc in next st) around. (42)
Rnd 8: <u>Working in back loops only</u>. Sc in each st around.
Rnd 9-15: Sc in each st around.
Rnd 16: <u>Working in front loops only</u>. (2 sc in next st, sc in next 2 sts) around. (56)
Rnd 17: (Sc in next 7 sts, 2 sc in next st) around. (63)
Rnd 18: Sc in each st around, sl st in first st, fasten off. (63)

Sew hat on top of head and stuff before sewing the opening close; sew free loops of rnd 15 of hat to the edge of hair to cover the top of head.

Nose

Rnd 1: With 2 strands of **Signal Red 977** and 5 mm hook, 6 sc in a magic ring. (6)
Rnd 2: 2 sc in each st around. (12)
Rnd 3: Sc next 2 sts tog around, join with sl st in first st, leave long end for sewing, fasten off.
Stuff nose, pin it on rnds 14 – 15 of head and sew.

Foot and Leg

Make one foot in **Baby Blue 854** color (rnds 1-21) and another foot in **Baby Mint 853** color (rnds 1-21).
Rnd 1: With 2 strands of **Baby Blue 854** color and 5 mm hook, 6 sc in a magic ring. (6)
Rnd 2: 2 sc in each st around. (12)
Rnd 3: (Sc in next st, 2 sc in next st) around. (18)
Rnd 4: (2 sc in next st, sc in next 2 sts) around. (24)
Rnd 5: Sc in each st around. (24)
Rnd 6: (Sc in next 7 sts, 2 sc in next st) around. (27)
Rnd 7: Sc in next 4 sts, 2 sc in next st, (sc in next 8 sts, 2 sc in next st) 2 times, sc in next 4 sts. (30)
Rnd 8: Sc in next 17 sts, sc next 2 sts tog, (sc in next 2sts, sc next 2 sts tog) 2 times, sc in next 3 sts. (27)
Rnd 9: Sc in each st around. (27)
Rnd 10: Sc in next 16 sts, sc next 2 sts tog, (sc in next st, sc next 2 sts tog) 2 times, sc in next 3 sts. (24)
Rnd 11: Sc in each st around. (24)
Rnd 12: Sc in next 15 sts, (sc next 2 sts tog) 3 times, sc in next 3 sts. (21)
Rnd 13: Sc in each st around. (21)

Rows 14-19 are working in Rows.
Row 14: Sc in next 15 sts, turn. (15)
Row 15: Ch 1, sc first 2 sts tog, sc in next 11 sts, sc next 2 sts tog, turn. (13)
Row 16: Ch 1, sc first 2 sts tog, sc in next 9 sts, sc next 2 sts tog, turn. (11)
Row 17: Ch 1, sc first 2 sts tog, sc in next 7 sts, sc next 2 sts tog, turn. (9)

Row 18: Ch 1, sc first 2 sts tog, sc in next 5 sts, sc next 2 sts tog, turn. (7)

Row 19: Ch 1, sc first 2 sts tog, sc in next 3 sts, sc next 2 sts tog, turn. (5)

Rnd 20-41 are working in continuous rounds.

Rnd 20: Working around the edge of foot, ch 1, sc next 2 sts tog, sc in next st, sc next 2 sts tog; working in ends of rows 14-19, (sc next 2 rows tog) 3 times; working in rnd 13, sc in next st, (sc next 2 sts tog) 2 times, sc in next st; working in ends of rows 15-19, sc in next row, (sc next 2 rows tog) 2 times. (13)

See how to crochet round 20 on page 8.

Rnd 21: Sc in next st, sc in next 2 sts tog, sc in next 3 sts, (sc next 2 sts tog) 2 times, sc in next 3 sts, changing to **Red** in last 2 loops of last st. Stuff foot. (10)

Rnd 22: Sc in each st around, changing to **White** in last 2 loops of last st.

Rnd 23: Sc in each st around, changing to **Red** in last 2 loops of last st.

Rnd 24: Sc in each st around, changing to **White** in last 2 loops of last st.

Rnd 25: Sc in each st around, changing to **Red** in last 2 loops of last st.

Rnd 26: Sc in each st around.

Rnd 27: Sc in each st around, changing to **Baby Lemon 852** in last 2 loops of last st.

Rnd 28: 2 sc in each st around. (20)

Rnd 29: (Sc in next 3 sts, 2 sc in next st) around. (25)

Rnd 30-40: Sc in each st around.

Rnd 41: Sc in each st around.

The first leg: join with sl st in first st, fasten off.
The second leg: do not sl st in first st, do not fasten off.

Body

With **Baby Lemon 852**, same as basic Huggy Body pattern on page 25.

Arm

Make 2 same as basic Huggy Arm pattern on page 26.
Rnds 1-9: color **Baby White 856**
Rnds 10-27: color **Baby Lemon 852**

Collar

Same as Collar pattern on page 27.
With colors **Baby White 856** and **Signal Red 977**, changing color in every 2 rows.

Button

Make 3; Blue, Green and Pink.

Rnd 1: With 2 strands of **Blue** and 5 mm hook, 6 sc in a magic ring, join with sl st in first st, leave long end for sewing, fasten off. (6)

Finishing

Sew head to the body. Sew arms to the body on rnd 25. Sew collar around the neck.
Sew three buttons on body as in picture.

Huggy Mermaid

Size
The Huggy Mermaids are 19.5 inches (49.5 cm) tall.

Materials
For making the Blue Huggy Mermaid.

- DK, Light Worsted
  Robin DK color:
  Cream 041 = 80 g and Royal 086 = 60 g
- Robin Paintbox DK color: Sapphire 235 = 60 g
- A little bit of Red embroidery thread
- 5.00 mm hook (US: H/8, UK: 6)
- Tapestry needle
- Polyester fibrefill = 200 g
- One pair of 12 mm safety eyes

Head
Make one the same as the basic Huggy Head pattern on page 24.

With **Red** embroidery thread embroider mouth.

Body
Starting from the neck, then crochet down to the tail.
Rnd 1: With 2 strands of **Cream** (skin color) and 5 mm hook, ch 18, sl st in the first chain to form a ring, ch 1, sc in each ch around. (18 sts made)
Rnd 2: Sc in each st around. (18)
Rnd 3: (Sc in next 2 sts, 2 sc in next st) around. (24)
Rnd 4: (2 sc in next st, sc in next 3 sts) around. (30)
Rnd 5-6: Sc in each st around.
Rnd 7: Sc in next 2 sts, 2 sc in next st, (sc in next 4 sts, 2 sc in next st) 5 times, sc in next 2 sts. (36)
Rnd 8-11: Sc in each st around.
Rnd 12: Sc in next 2 sts, sc next 2 sts tog, (sc in next 4 sts, sc next 2 sts tog) 5 times, sc in next 2 sts. (30)
Rnd 13: (Sc in next 3 sts, sc next 2 sts tog) around. (24)
Rnd 14: Sc in each st around.
Rnd 15: (Sc in next 3 sts, 2 sc in next st) around. (30)
Rnd 16: Sc in next 2 sts, 2 sc in next st, (sc in next 4 sts, 2 sc in next st) 5 times, sc in next 2 sts. (36)
Rnd 17: Sc in each st around, changing to **Sapphire 235** (tail color) in last 2 loops of last st.
Rnd 18: (Sc in next 5 sts, 2 sc in next st) around. (42)

Rounds 19 – 51 are working in back loops only.

Rnd 19: Sc in each st around.
Rnd 20: Sc in next 3 sts, 2 sc in next st, (sc in next 6 sts, 2 sc in next st) 5 times, sc in next 3 sts. (48)
Rnd 21-24: Sc in each st around.
Rnd 25: Sc in next 7 sts, sc next 2 sts tog, (sc in next 14 sts, sc next 2 sts tog) 2 times, sc in next 7 sts. (45)
Rnd 26: Sc in each st around.
Rnd 27: (Sc in next 13 sts, sc next 2 sts tog) around. (42)
Rnd 28: Sc in each st around.
Rnd 29: Sc in next 6 sts, sc next 2 sts tog, (sc in next 12 sts, sc next 2 sts tog) 2 times, sc in next 6 sts. (39)
Rnd 30: Sc in each st around.
Rnd 31: (Sc in next 11 sts, sc next 2 sts tog) around. (36)
Rnd 32: Sc in each st around.
Rnd 33: Sc in next 5 sts, sc next 2 sts tog, (sc in next 10 sts, sc next 2 sts tog) 2 times, sc in next 5 sts. (33)
Rnd 34: Sc in each st around.
Rnd 35: (Sc in next 9 sts, sc next 2 sts tog) around. (30)
Rnd 36: Sc in each st around.
Rnd 37: Sc in next 4 sts, sc next 2 sts tog, (sc in next 8 sts, sc next 2 sts tog) 2 times, sc in next 4 sts. (27)
Rnd 38: Sc in each st around.
Rnd 39: (Sc in next 7 sts, sc next 2 sts tog) around. (24)

Rnd 40: Sc in each st around.
Rnd 41: Sc in next 3 sts, sc next 2 sts tog, (sc in next 6 sts, sc next 2 sts tog) 2 times, sc in next 3 sts. (21)
Rnd 42: Sc in each st around.
Rnd 43: (Sc in next 5 sts, sc next 2 sts tog) around. (18)
Rnd 44: Sc in each st around.
Rnd 45: Sc in next 2 sts, sc next 2 sts tog, (sc in next 4 sts, sc next 2 sts tog) 2 times, sc in next 2 sts. (15)
Rnd 46: Sc in each st around.
Rnd 47: (Sc in next 3 sts, sc next 2 sts tog) around. (12)
Rnd 48: Sc in each st around.
Rnd 49: (Sc in next 2 sts, sc next 2 sts tog) around. (9)
Rnd 50: Sc in each st around.
Rnd 51: (Sc in next st, sc next 2 sts tog) around. (6)

Rnd 52: **Tail**; 2sc in each st around. (12)
Rnd 53: 2 sc in each st around. (24)
Rnd 54: Sc in each st around. (24)
Rnd 55: (Sc in next 3 sts, 2 sc in next st) around. (30)
Rnd 56: First half of tail; sc in next 15 sts, skip 15 sts. (15) The picture below shows the finished rnd 56.

Rnd 57-58: Sc in each st around. (15)
Rnd 59: (Sc in next 3 sts, sc next 2 sts tog) around. (12)
Rnd 60: Sc in each st around. (12)
Rnd 61: (Sc in next 2 sts, sc next 2 sts tog) around. (9)
Rnd 62: Sc in each st around. (9)
Rnd 63: (Sc in next st, sc next 2 sts tog) around. (6)
Rnd 64: Sc next 2 sts tog around,
join with sl st in first st, fasten off. (3)

Rnd 56: Second half of tail; join 2 strands of **Sapphire 235** (tail color) in the st next to the first half of tail on rnd 55, sc in next 15 sts. (15)

Rnd 57-58: Sc in each st around. (15)
Rnd 59: (Sc in next 3 sts, sc next 2 sts tog) around. (12)
Rnd 60: Sc in each st around. (12)
Rnd 61: (Sc in next 2 sts, sc next 2 sts tog) around. (9)
Rnd 62: Sc in each st around. (9)
Rnd 63: (Sc in next st, sc next 2 sts tog) around. (6)
Rnd 64: Sc next 2 sts tog around, join with sl st in first st, fasten off. (3)

Stuff the body and sew to the head.

Arm
Make 2.
Rnd 1: With **Cream**, 6 sc in a magic ring. (6)
Rnd 2: 2 sc in each st around. (12)
Rnd 3: (Sc in next st, 2 sc in next st) around. (18)
Rnd 4-6: Sc in each st around. (18)
Rnd 7: (Sc next 2 sts tog, sc in next 4 sts) around. (15)
Rnd 8: (Sc in next 3 sts, sc next 2 sts tog) around. (12)
Rnd 9: (Sc in next 2 sts, sc next 2 sts tog) around.
Stuff. (9)
Rnd 10-26: Sc in each st around.

Rnd 27: Sc in each st around, sl st in first st, leave long end for sewing, fasten off.

Sew arms to rnd 4 of the body.

Bra

First cup: working in rows
Row 1: With 2 strands of **Sapphire 235** and
5 mm hook, ch 13, sc in second chain from hook,
sc in next 5 chs, turn. (6)
Row 2: Ch 1, sc first 2 sts tog, sc in next 2 sts, sc next 2
sts tog, turn. (4)
Row 3: Ch 1, sc first 2 sts tog, sc next 2 sts tog, turn. (2)
Row 4: Ch 1, sc first 2 sts tog, ch 30, fasten off.
(1 sc, 30 chs)

Second cup
Row 1: Join 2 strands of **Sapphire 235** in the chain next
to the first cup, sc in next 6 sts, turn. (6)

Row 2: Ch 1, sc first 2 sts tog, sc in next 2 sts, sc next 2
sts tog, turn. (4)
Row 3: Ch 1, sc first 2 sts tog, sc next 2 sts tog, turn. (2)

Row 4: Ch 1, sc first 2 sts tog, ch 30, fasten off.
(1 sc, 30 chs)

Body strap: with 2 strands of **Royal 086** and 5 mm hook,
ch 30, sc in the bottom of bra; sc in next 12 sts, ch 30,
fasten off. (30 chs, 12 sc, 30 chs)

Hair

Rnd 1: With **Royal 086** (hair color), 6 sc in a magic ring. (6 sc made)
Rnd 2: 2 sc in each st around. (12)
Rnd 3: (Sc in next st, 2 sc in next st) around. (18)
Rnd 4: (2 sc in next st, sc in next 2 sts) around. (24)
Rnd 5: (Sc in next 3 sts, 2 sc in next st) around. (30)
Rnd 6: Sc in next 2 sts, 2 sc in next st, (sc in next 4 sts, 2 sc next st) 5 times, sc in next 2 sts. (36)
Rnd 7: (Sc in next 5 sts, 2 sc in next st) around. (42)
Rnd 8: Sc in next 3 sts, 2 sc in next st, (sc in next 6 sts, 2 sc in next st) 5 times, sc in next 3 sts. (48)
Rnd 9: (Sc in next 7 sts, 2 sc in next st) around. (54)
Rnd 10: Sc in next 4 sts, 2 sc in next st, (sc in next 8 sts, 2 sc in next st) 5 times, sc in next 4 sts. (60)
Rnd 11: (Sc in next 19 sts, 2 sc in next st) around. (63)
Rnd 12-17: Sc in each st around.

Rows 18 – 19 are working in rows.
Row 18: Sc in next 46 sts, turn. (46)
Row 19: Curly hair; (ch 30, 2 sc in second ch from hook, 2 sc in next 28 chs, skip 2 sts on row 19, sl st in next st on row 19) 15 times, fasten off.

Finishing

Put hair on head and sew.
Put bra on Mermaid.

Huggy Tiger

Size

Huggy Tiger is 17.5 inches (44.5 cm) tall, excluding ears.

Materials

- DK, Light Worsted
  Sirdar Hayfield Bonus Baby DK color:
  Baby Mint 853 = 50 g and
  Baby White 856 = 50g
  Sirdar Hayfield Bonus DK color:
  Peach 736 = 100 g and Grey 838 = 35 g
- 5.00 mm hook (US: H/8, UK: 6)
- Tapestry needle
- Polyester fibrefill = 250 g
- One pair of 12mm safety eyes

Head

Rnd 1: With 2 strands of **Peach 736** and 5 mm hook, 6 sc in a magic ring. (6)

Rnd 2: 2 sc in each st around. (12)

Rnd 3: (2 sc in next st, sc in next st) around, changing to **Grey 838** in last 2 loops of last st. (18)

Rnd 4: (Sc in next 2 sts, 2 sc in next st) around, changing to **Peach** in last 2 loops of last st. (24)

Rnd 5: (Sc in next 3 sts, 2 sc in next st) around. (30)

Rnd 6: Sc in next 2 sts, 2 sc in next st, (sc in next 4 sts, 2 sc in next st) 5 times, sc in next 2 sts. (36)

Rnd 7: (Sc in next 5 sts, 2 sc in next st) around, changing to **Grey** in last 2 loops of last st. (42)

Rnd 8: Sc in next 3 sts, 2 sc in next st, (sc in next 6 sts, 2 sc in next st) 5 times, sc in next 3 sts, changing to **Peach** in last 2 loops of last st. (48)

Rnd 9: (Sc in next 7 sts, 2 sc in next st) around. (54)

Rnd 10: Sc in next 4 sts, 2 sc in next st, (sc in next 8 sts, 2 sc in next st) 5 times, sc in next 4 sts. (60)

Rnd 11: Sc in each st around, changing to **Grey** in last 2 loops of last st.

Rnd 12: Sc in next 23 sts, changing to **Peach**; sc in next 22 sts, changing to **Grey**; sc in next 15 sts, changing to **Peach** in last 2 loops of last st. (60)

Rnd 13-14: Sc in each st around.

Rnd 15: Sc in each st around, changing to **Grey** in last 2 loops of last st.

Rnd 16: Sc in next 23 sts, changing to **Peach**; sc in next 23 sts, changing to **Grey**; sc in next 14 sts, changing to **Peach** in last 2 loops of last st. (60)

Rnd 17: (Sc next 2 sts tog, sc in next 8 sts) around. (54)

Rnd 18: (Sc in next 7 sts, sc next 2 sts tog) around. (48)

Rnd 19: Sc in next 3 sts, sc next 2 sts tog, (sc in next 6 sts, sc next 2 sts tog) 5 times, sc in next 3 sts, changing to **Grey** in last 2 loops of last st. (42)

Rnd 20: (Sc next 2 sts tog, sc in next 5 sts) around, changing to **Peach** in last 2 loops of last st. (36)

Rnd 21: Sc in next 2 sts, sc next 2 sts tog, (sc in next 4 sts, sc next 2 sts tog) 5 times, sc in next 2 sts. (30)

Rnd 22: (Sc in next 3 sts, sc next 2 sts tog) around. (24)

Rnd 23: (Sc in next 2 sts, sc next 2 sts tog) around, join with sl st in first st, fasten off. (18)

Stuff head a little bit, insert safety eyes 10 sts apart between rnds 13-14 of head then stuff head more tightly.

Foot and Leg

Make 2 same as basic huggy foot and leg pattern on page 24.

Rnds 1-21: color **Peach 736**.

Rnds 22-41: crochet one strand of **Baby Mint 853** and one strand of **Baby White 856** together.

Body

Crochet one strand of **Baby Mint 853** and one strand of **Baby White 856** together. The pattern is the same as the basic huggy body pattern on page 25.

Arm

Make 2 the same as basic huggy arm pattern on page 26.

Rnds 1-9: color **Peach 736**

Rnds 10-27: crochet one strand of **Baby Mint 853** and one strand of **Baby White 856** together.

Collar

Crochet one strand of **Baby Mint 853** and one strand of **Baby White 856** together, pattern same as collar pattern on page 27.

Tail

Rnd 1: With **Grey**, 5 sc in a magic ring. (5)

Rnd 2: Sc in each st around. (5)

Rnd 3: Sc in each st around, changing to **Peach** in last 2 loops of last st. (5)

Rnd 4: Sc in each st around. (5)

Rnd 5: Sc in each st around, changing to **Grey** in last 2 loops of last st. (5)

Rnd 6: Sc in each st around, changing to **Peach** in last 2 loops of last st. (5)

Rnd 7: Sc in each st around. (5)

Rnd 8: Sc in each st around, changing to **Grey** in last 2 loops of last st. (5)

Rnd 9: Sc in each st around, changing to **Peach** in last 2 loops of last st. (5)

Rnd 10: Sc in each st around. (5)

Rnd 11: Sc in each st around, changing to **Grey** in last 2 loops of last st. (5)

Rnd 12: Sc in each st around, changing to **Peach** in last 2 loops of last st. (5)

Rnd 13: Sc in each st around. (5)

Rnd 14: Sc in each st around, changing to **Grey** in last 2 loops of last st. (5)

Rnd 15: Sc in each st around, changing to **Peach** in last 2 loops of last st. (5)

Rnd 16: Sc in each st around. (5)

Rnd 17: Sc in each st around, changing to **Grey** in last 2 loops of last st. (5)

Rnd 18: Sc in each st around, changing to **Peach** in last 2 loops of last st. (5)
Rnd 19: Sc in each st around. (5)
Rnd 20: Sc in each st around, sl st in first st, leave long end for sewing, fasten off. (5)

Sew ears on rnds 5-11 of the head.

Sew tail to rnds 6-7 of the body.

Ear

Make 2.
Rnd 1: With **Peach 736**, 6 sc in a magic ring. (6)
Rnd 2: 2 sc in each st around. (12)
Rnd 3: (2 sc in next st, sc in next st) around. (18)
Rnd 4-5: Sc in each st around. (18)
Rnd 6: (Sc next 2 sts tog, sc in next 4 sts) around, join with sl st in first st. Leave long end for sewing, fasten off. (15)

Huggy Leo

Size
Huggy Leo is 19 inches (48 cm) tall, including hair.

Materials
- DK, Light Worsted
  Sirdar Hayfield Bonus Baby DK color:
  Baby Lemon 852 = 50g and
  Baby Lilac 850 = 100g
  Robin DK color: **Lavender 053** = 30 g and
  Sunflower 075 = 50 g
- 5.00 mm and 3.00 mm hooks
- DMC Pearl Cotton Thread Size 3 color Orange 740
- Tapestry needle
- Polyester fibrefill = 250 g
- One pair of 12mm safety eyes

Head
With **Baby Lemon 852**, make one same as basic huggy head pattern on page 24.

Ear
Make 2.
Rnd 1: With **Baby Lemon 852**, 6 sc in a magic ring. (6)
Rnd 2: 2 sc in each st around. (12)
Rnd 3: (2 sc in next st, sc in next st) around. (18)
Rnd 4: Sc in each st around. (18)
Rnd 5: (Sc next 2 sts tog, sc in next 4 sts) around, join with sl st in first st. Leave long end for sewing, fasten off. (15)

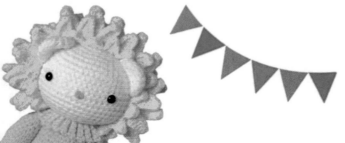

Pin ears to rnds 6-12 of head and sew.

Nose
With DMC Pearl Cotton Thread Size 3 color **Orange 740**, same as basic animal nose pattern on page 27.

Foot and Leg
Make 2 same as basic huggy foot and leg pattern on page 24.
Rnds 1-21: color **Lavender 053**.
Rnds 22-41: color **Baby Lilac 850**.

Body
With **Baby Lilac 850**, same as basic huggy body pattern on page 25.

Arm
Make 2 same as basic huggy arm pattern on page 26.
Rnds 1-9: color **Baby Lemon 852**.
Rnds 10-27: color **Baby Lilac 850**.

Hair

Make 2 each of: Big hair line, Medium hair line and Small hair line (total 6 hair lines).

Big hair line

Step 1: With 2 strands of **Sunflower 075** and 5 mm hook, (ch 9, sl st in second chain from hook, sl st in next ch, sc in next 2 chs, hdc in next 2 chs, dc in next 2 chs) 12 times, turn.

Medium hair line

Step 1: With 2 strands of **Sunflower 075** and 5 mm hook, (ch 7, sl st in second chain from hook, sc in next ch, hdc in next 2 chs, dc in next 2 chs) 11 times, turn.
Step 2: Sl st in both long sides of triangle.

Small hair line

Step 1: With 2 strands of **Sunflower 075** and 5 mm hook, (ch 5, sl st in second chain from hook, sc in next ch, hdc in next ch, dc in next ch) 14 times, turn.
Step 2: Sl st in both long sides of triangle.

Sew or crochet (using sc stitch) one big and one medium hair lines together, see picture below.
Do the same with the other big and medium hair line.

Step 2: Sl st in both long sides of triangle, see picture below.

Sayjai Amigurumi

Pin one set of big and medium hair line behind the ears with the medium hair line facing the front. Sew to the head.

Pin the small hair line in front of medium hair line on the back and sew to head.

Pin another set of big and medium hair line behind the first set with the medium hair line facing the back (2 big hair lines are in the middle). Sew to the head.

Collar

With colors **Baby Lilac 850**, same as Collar pattern on page 27.

Tail

Row 1: With 2 strands of **Baby Lemon 852** and 5 mm hook, ch 30, sc in second ch from hook, sc in each st across, turn. (29)

Row 2: Ch 1, sc in each st across, leave long end for sewing, fasten off. (29)

Pin the small hair line behind ears and in front of medium hair line and sew to head.

Sew top and bottom edge together, see pictures below.

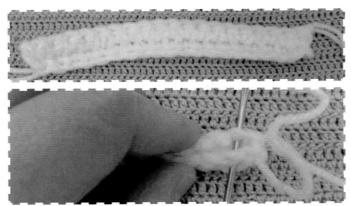

Making fluffy hair at the end of tail.
Cut 10 pieces of yarn about 3 inches long. Attaching the yarn: fold one piece of yarn in half, insert the hook at the end of tail pull out the loop, put both end of yarn in the loop and pull tight. Repeat attaching the yarn until finish all yarn.

Sew tail to rnd 7 of the body.

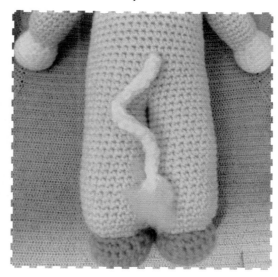

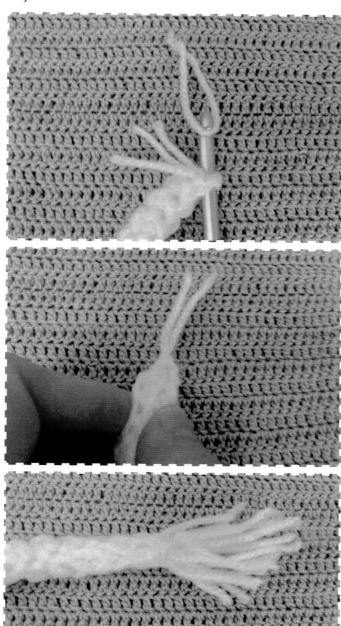

Brush the end of tail with yarn indicator brush or use the tip of needle to split the yarn.

Huggy Mousey

Size

Huggy Mousey is 17.5 inches (44.5 cm) tall, excluding ears.

Materials

- DK, Light Worsted **3 Light**
  Sirdar Hayfield Bonus Baby DK color:
  Baby Rose 867 = 40 g and
  Baby Pink 851 = 100 g
  Sirdar Hayfield Bonus DK color
  Silver Grey 838 = 60 g
- 5.00 mm and 3.00 mm hook
- DMC Pearl Cotton Thread Size 3 color
  Pink 3326
- Tapestry needle
- Polyester fibrefill = 250 g
- One pair of 12mm safety eyes
- Three 10 mm heart buttons for decoration
- Needle and thread for sewing buttons

Head

With **Silver Grey 838**, make one same as basic huggy head pattern on page 24.

Foot and Leg

Make 2 same as basic huggy foot and leg pattern on page 24.
Rnds 1-21: color **Baby Rose 867**
Rnds 22-41: color **Baby Pink 851**

Body

With **Baby Pink 851**, same as basic huggy body pattern on page 25.

Arm

Make 2 same as basic huggy arm pattern on page 26.
Rnds 1-9: color **Silver Grey 838**
Rnds 10-27: color **Baby Pink 851**

Collar

Same as Collar pattern on page 27.
With colors **Baby Pink 851** and **Baby Rose 867**, changing color in every 2 rows.

Ear

Make 2 in Grey color and 2 in Baby Pink color.
Rnd 1: With 2 strands of **Baby Pink 851** and 5 mm hook, 6 sc in a magic ring. (6)
Rnd 2: 2 sc in each st around. (12)
Rnd 3: (2 sc in next st, sc in next st) around. (18)
Rnd 4: (Sc in next 2 sts, 2 sc in next st) around, join with sl st in first st, fasten off. (24)

Rnd 5: Matching sts, hold one **Pink** ear and one **Grey** ear together. With **Pink** side facing you, join **Grey** on rnd 4 through both thicknesses, ch 1, sc in same st, sc in each st around. (24)

Rnd 6: Sl st in each st around, leave long end for sewing, fasten off. (24)

Pin ears on rnds 6-8 of head and sew.

Mouse Tail

With **Silver Grey**, ch 30, sl st in second chain from hook, sl st in next 4 chs, sc in next 10 chs, hdc in next 10 chs, dc in next 4 chs, leave long end for sewing, fasten off. (29 sts made)

Sew top and bottom of the row together, see pictures.

Sew tail to rnd 6 of the body.

Nose

With DMC Pearl Cotton Thread Size 3 color **Pink 3326**, make one same as basic animal nose pattern on page 27.
Sew nose on rnd 14 between eyes.
Sew buttons on the body.

Huggy Lamby

Size

Huggy Lamby is 17.5 inches (44.5 cm) tall.

Materials

- DK, Light Worsted
  Sirdar Hayfield Bonus DK color:
  Peachy 736 = 100 g,
  Punchy Pink 728 = 30 g and
  Wheat 816 = 80 g

- Bulky, Chunky
  Schachenmayr Nomotta Cassiopeia
  color White = 50 g (or use Sirdar
  Snugly Snowflake Chunky)
- 5.00 mm hook and 3 mm hook
- DMC Pearl Cotton Thread Size 3 color
  Orange 740
- Tapestry needle
- Polyester fibrefill = 250 g
- One pair of 12mm safety eyes

Head

Rnd 1: With 2 strands of **Wheat 816** and 5
mm hook, 6 sc in a magic ring. (6)

Rnds 2-11 are working in back loops only.

Rnd 2: 2 sc in each st around. (12)
Rnd 3: (2 sc in next st, sc in next st)
around. (18)
Rnd 4: (Sc in next 2 sts, 2 sc in next st)
around. (24)
Rnd 5: (Sc in next 3 sts, 2 sc in next st)
around. (30)
Rnd 6: Sc in next 2 sts, 2 sc in next st,
(sc in next 4 sts, 2 sc in next st) 5 times,
sc in next 2 sts. (36)
Rnd 7: (Sc in next 5 sts, 2 sc in next st)
around. (42)

Rnd 8: Sc in next 3 sts, 2 sc in next st, (sc in next 6 sts, 2 sc in next st) 5 times, sc in next 3 sts. (48)
Rnd 9: (Sc in next 7 sts, 2 sc in next st) around. (54)
Rnd 10: Sc in next 4 sts, 2 sc in next st, (sc in next 8 sts, 2 sc in next st) 5 times, sc in next 4 sts. (60)
Rnd 11: Sc in each st around. (60)

Rnd 12-16: Sc in each st around. (60)
Rnd 17: (Sc next 2 sts tog, sc in next 8 sts) around. (54)
Rnd 18: (Sc in next 7 sts, sc next 2 sts tog) around. (48)
Rnd 19: Sc in next 3 sts, sc next 2 sts tog, (sc in next 6 sts, sc next 2 sts tog) 5 times, sc in next 3 sts. (42)
Rnd 20: (Sc in next 5 sts, sc next 2 sts tog) around. (36)
Rnd 21: Sc in next 2 sts, sc next 2 sts tog, (sc in next 4 sts, sc next 2 sts tog) 5 times, sc in next 2 sts. (30)
Rnd 22: (Sc in next 3 sts, sc next 2 sts tog) around. (24)
Rnd 23: (Sc in next 2 sts, sc next 2 sts tog) around, join with sl st in first st, fasten off. (18)

Hair on top of head.

Join Schachenmayr nomotta Cassiopeia color **White** to a free loop on middle top of head, ch 1, sc in same st, sc in every free loops, fasten off.

Stuff head a little bit, insert safety eyes 10 sts apart between rnds 13-14 of head then stuff head more tightly.

Nose

With DMC Pearl Cotton color **Orange 740**, make one same as basic animal nose pattern on page 27.

Foot and Leg

Make 2 same as basic huggy foot and leg pattern on page 24.
Rnds 1-21: color **Punchy Pink 728**.
Rnds 22-41: color **Peachy 736**.

Body

With **Peachy 736**, make one same as basic huggy body pattern on page 25.

Arm

Make 2 same as basic huggy arm pattern on page 26.
Rnds 1-9: color **Wheat 816**.
Rnds 10-27: color **Peachy 736**.

Ear

Make 2.
Rnd 1: With 2 strands of **Wheat 816** and 5 mm hook, 6 sc in a magic ring. (6)
Rnd 2: (Sc in next st, 2 sc in next st) around. (9)
Rnd 3: (2 sc in next st, sc in next 2 sts) around. (12)
Rnd 4: (Sc in next st, 2 sc in next st) around. (18)
Rnd 5: (2 sc in next st, sc in next 2 sts) around. (24)
Rnd 6-8: Sc in each st around.
Rnd 9: (Sc in next 2 sts, sc next 2 sts tog) around. (18)
Rnd 10-12: Sc in each st around.
Rnd 13: (Sc next 2 sts tog, sc in next 4 sts) around. (15)
Rnd 14: Sc in each st around.
Rnd 15: (Sc in next 3 sts, sc next 2 sts tog) around. (12)
Rnd 16: (Sc next 2 sts tog, sc in next 2 sts) around, join with sl st in first st. Leave long end for sewing, fasten off. (9)

Sew the opening close flat.

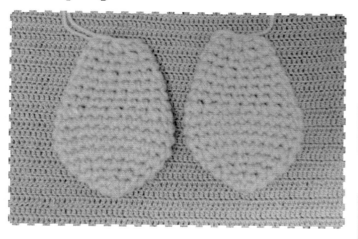

Sew ears on rnd 12 of head.

Collar

Same as Collar pattern on page 27.
With colors **Punchy Pink 728** and **Peachy 736**, changing color in every 2 rows.

Huggy Doggy

Size

Huggy Doggy is 17.5 inches (44.5 cm) tall.

Materials

- DK, Light Worsted ![3 Light]
  Sirdar Hayfield Bonus DK color:
  Silver Grey 838 = 30 g, Grass 825 = 30 g,
  Lime 882 = 70 g, Wheat 816 = 60 g and
  Walnut 927 = 30 g
- 5.00 mm hook and 3 mm hook
- DMC Pearl Cotton Thread Size 3 color Black 310
- Tapestry needle
- Polyester fibrefill = 250 g
- One pair of 12mm safety eyes

Head

With **Wheat 816**, make one same as basic huggy head pattern on page 24.

Foot and Leg

Make 2 same as basic huggy foot and leg pattern on page 24.
Rnds 1-21: color **Grass 825**.
Rnds 22-41: The main color is **Lime 882** and has grey stripes (color **Silver Grey 838**) on rnds 24, 27, 30, 33, 36 and 39.

Body

Same as basic huggy body pattern on page 25.
The main color is **Lime 882** and has grey stripes (color **Silver Grey 838**) on rnds 1, 4, 7, 10, 13, 16, 19, 22 and 25.

Arm

Make 2 same as basic huggy arm pattern on page 26.
Rnds 1-9: color **Wheat 816**.
Rnds 10-27: The main color is **Lime 882** color and has grey stripes (color **Silver Grey 838**) on rnds 12, 15, 18, 21, 24 and 27.

Collar

With **Silver Grey 838**, same as Collar pattern on page 27.

Nose

With DMC Pearl Cotton Thread Size 3 color **Black 310**, make one same as basic animal nose pattern on page 27.

Ear

Make 2.
Rnd 1: With 2 strands of **Walnut 927** and 5 mm hook, 6 sc in a magic ring. (6)
Rnd 2: 2 sc in each st around. (12)
Rnd 3: (2 sc in next st, sc in next st) around. (18)
Rnd 4: (Sc in next 2 sts, 2 sc in next st) around. (24)
Rnd 5-7: Sc in each st around.
Rnd 8: (Sc in next 2 sts, sc next 2 sts tog) around. (18)
Rnd 9-11: Sc in each st around.
Rnd 12: (Sc next 2 sts tog, sc in next 4 sts) around. (15)
Rnd 13: Sc in each st around.
Rnd 14: (Sc in next 3 sts, sc next 2 sts tog) around. (12)
Rnd 15-16: Sc in each st around.
Rnd 17: Sc in each st around, join with sl st in first st.
Leave long end for sewing, fasten off.
Sew the opening close flat. Sew ears to rnd 11 of head.

Snowy Bunny

Size
Snowy Bunny is 17.5 inches (44.5 cm) tall.

Materials

- DK, Light Worsted **[3 Light]**
  Sirdar Hayfield Bonus Baby DK color:
  Baby Pink 851 = 70 g, Baby Mint 853 = 20 g
  and Baby White 856 = 135 g
- 5.00 mm hook
- Tapestry needle
- Polyester fibrefill = 250 g
- One pair of 12mm safety eyes

Foot and Leg
Make 2 same as basic huggy foot and leg
pattern on page 24.
Rnds 1-21: color **Baby White 856**.
Rnds 22-41: The main color is **Baby Pink 851**
with light green stripes on rnds 24, 27, 30, 33, 36
and 39. For the light green stripes crochet one
strand of **Baby Mint 853** and one strand of **Baby
White 856** together.

Body
Same as basic huggy body pattern on page 25.
The main color is **Baby Pink 851** and has light
green stripes (crochet one strand of **Baby Mint
853** and one strand of **Baby White 856** together)
on rnds 1, 4, 7, 10, 13, 16, 19, 22 and 25.

Arm
Make 2 same as basic huggy arm pattern on
page 26.
Rnds 1-9: color **Baby White 856**.
Rnds 10-27: The main color is **Baby Pink 851**
and has light green stripes (crochet one strand of
Baby Mint 853 and one strand of **Baby White
856** together) on rnds 12, 15, 18, 21, 24 and 27.

Head

With **Baby White 856**, make one the same as the basic huggy head pattern on page 24.

Ear

Make 2.

Rnd 1: With 2 strands of **Baby White 856** and 5 mm hook, 6 sc in a magic ring. (6)
Rnd 2: (Sc in next st, 2 sc in next st) around. (9)
Rnd 3: (2 sc in next st, sc in next 2 sts) around. (12)
Rnd 4: (Sc in next 3 sts, 2 sc in next st) around. (15)
Rnd 5: Sc in next 2 sts, 2 sc in next st, (sc in next 4 sts, 2 sc in next st) 2 times, sc in next 2 sts. (18)
Rnd 6: (Sc in next 5 sts, 2 sc in next st) around. (21)
Rnd 7: Sc in next 3 sts, 2 sc in next st, (sc in next 6 sts, 2 sc in next st) 2 times, sc in next 3 sts. (24)
Rnd 8: (Sc in next 7 sts, 2 sc in next st) around. (27)
Rnd 9-15: Sc in each st around.
Rnd 16: (Sc next 2 sts tog, sc in next 7 sts) around. (24)
Rnd 17-18: Sc in each st around.
Rnd 19: Sc in next 3 sts, sc next 2 sts tog, (sc in next 6 sts, sc next 2 sts tog) 2 times, sc in next 3 sts. (21)
Rnd 20-21: Sc in each st around.
Rnd 22: (Sc next 2 sts tog, sc in next 5 sts) around. (18)
Rnd 23-24: Sc in each st around.
Rnd 25: Sc in next 2 sts, sc next 2 sts tog, (sc in next 4 sts, sc next 2 sts tog) 2 times, sc in next 2 sts. (15)
Rnd 26-27: Sc in each st around.
Rnd 28: (Sc next 2 sts tog, sc in next 3 sts) around. (12)
Rnd 29-30: Sc in each st around.
Rnd 31: (Sc in next 2 sts, sc next 2 sts tog) around. (9)
Rnd 32-33: Sc in each st around.
Rnd 34: (Sc next 2 sts tog, sc in next st) around. (6)
Rnd 35: Sc in each st around, join with sl st in first st. Leave long end for sewing, fasten off. (6)
Sew ears on rnd 10 of head.

Collar

With **Baby Pink 851** color, same as Collar pattern on page 27.

Bow

Bow

Row 1: With 2 strands of **Baby Pink 851** and 5 mm hook, ch 10, sc in second ch from hook, sc in next 8 chs, turn. (9)

Rows 2-6 are working in back loops only.

Row 2-5: Ch 1, sc in each st across, turn. (9)
Row 6: Ch 1, sc in each st across, fasten off. (9)

Middle piece Ch 6, sc in second ch from hook, sc in next 4 chs, leave long end for sewing, fasten off. (5)

Sew the middle piece around the bow.
Sew the bow on head.

Yarn Weight System				
	USA	UK	Australia	Recommended Hook in Metric (mm)
0 Lace	Lace weight	1 ply	2 ply	1.5 - 2.25 mm
1 Super Fine	Fingering	2 ply	3 ply	2.25 - 3 mm
	Sock	3 ply	3 ply	2.25 - 3.5 mm
2 Fine	Sport	4 ply	5 ply	3.5 - 4.5 mm
3 Light	DK, Light worsted	DK	8 ply	4.5 - 5.5 mm
4 Medium	Worsted	Aran	10 ply	5.5 - 6.5 mm
5 Bulky	Bulky	Chunky	12 ply	6.5 - 9 mm
6 Super Bulky	Super Bulky	Super Chunky	14 ply	9 mm and larger

Crochet Hook Size Conversion			
Hook in Metric (mm)	USA	UK	Japanese
1.00 mm	10 steel	4 steel	4 steel
1.25 mm	8 steel	3 steel	2 steel
1.50 mm	7 steel	2.5 steel	--
1.75 mm	4 steel	2 steel	--
2.00 mm	--	14	2/0
2.25 mm	B/1	13	3/0
2.50 mm	--	12	4/0
2.75 mm	C/2	--	--
3.00 mm	--	11	5/0
3.25 mm	D/3	10	--
3.50 mm	E/4	9	6/0
3.75 mm	F/5	--	--
4.00 mm	G/6	8	7/0
4.50 mm	7	7	7.5/0
5.00 mm	H/8	6	8/0
5.50 mm	I/9	5	--
6.00 mm	J/10	4	10/0
6.50 mm	K/10.5	3	7
7.00 mm	--	2	--
8.00 mm	L/11	0	8
9.00 mm	M/13	00	9
10.00 mm	N/15	000	10

Copyright

First Edition
ISBN: 978-1-910407-41-7
Date of publication: April 30th 2016
Editor: Robert Appelboom
Cover design: Maria K. Windayani

Publisher: K and J Publishing
16 Whitegate Close
Swavesey, Cambridge CB24 4TT
United Kingdom
e-mail: kandjdolls@gmail.com

Huggy Dolls Amigurumi
Subtitle: 15 Huggable Doll Patterns
Publisher: K and J Publishing
Author: Sayjai Thawornsupacharoen
Publication date: 14th of June 2014
ISBN: 978-1910407028

Easy Amigurumi
Subtitle: 28 doll patterns
Publisher: K and J Publishing
Author: Sayjai Thawornsupacharoen
Publication date: 18th of July 2014
ISBN: 978-1910407011

Dress Up Dolls Amigurumi
Subtitle: 5 big dolls with clothes, shoes, accessories, tiny bear and big carry bag patterns
Publisher: K and J Publishing
Author: Sayjai Thawornsupacharoen
Publication date: September 27th 2014
ISBN: 978-1910407066

Sunny Amigurumi
Subtitle: Crochet Patterns
Publisher: K and J Publishing
Author: Sayjai Thawornsupacharoen
Editor: Robert Appelboom
Publication date: February 25th 2015
ISBN: 978-1910407189

Kawaii Amigurumi
28 Cute Animal Crochet Patterns
Publisher: K and J Publishing
Author: Sayjai Thawornsupacharoen
Publication date: June 27th 2015
ISBN: 978-1910407264

Christmas Amigurumi
Crochet Patterns
Publisher: K and J Publishing
Author: Sayjai Thawornsupacharoen
Publication date: November 19th 2015
ISBN: 978-1910407318

Sayjai's next pattern book will be a
story book for children about little
Cushie, Cushionette and all their friends.
The book will have clear crochet patterns
to make Cushie and her friends yourself.

Made in the USA
Middletown, DE
14 September 2021